MY ALPHABET BOOK
MI LIBRO ALFABÉTO

Aa
Avocado

A is for avocado.

Aguacate - A como en el aguacate.

SHARON ANN DUVERNAY, ED.D.
ILLUSTRATED BY ROGELIO ASTORGA

COVER DESIGN BY JOHN SIBLEY

My Alphabet Book – Mi Libro Alfabéto

Copyright 2012 by Sharon Ann Duvernay, Ed. D.

All rights reserved. No part of this book may be reproduced by any mechanical, photographic, or electronic process, or in the form of a phonographic recording; nor may it be stored in a retrieval system, transmitted, or otherwise be copied for public or private use without written permission from the publisher.

For information regarding permission or additional copies, contact publisher:

KNOWLEDGE POWER BOOKS
A Division of Knowledge Power Communications, Inc.
25379 Wayne Mills Place, Suite 131, Valencia, CA 91355
661 513 0308 F 661 513 0381 www.knowledgepowerbooks.com

ISBN: 978-0-9888644-0-5
Library of Congress Control Number: 2013930463

Cover and Interior Design:
John Sibley
Rock Solid Productions
www.rocksoilidgraphicarts.com

Printed in the United States of America

Dedication

This book is dedicated to children everywhere.
May your days overflow with love, support and respect.
May your nights contain only the sweetest dreams.
And when you awaken refreshed each brand new day,
know the world is a better place because of you.

Aa

Avocado   A is for avocado.

Aguacate   A como en el aguacate.

Bb

Bananas   B is for bananas.

Bananas   B como en los bananas.

Cc

Coconut   C is for coconut.

Coco   C como en el coco.

Ch

Chimpancé   Ch como en el chimpancé.

Dd

Doughnuts   D is for doughnuts.

Donas   D como en las donas.

Ee

Elephant   E is for elephant.

Elefante   E como en el elefante.

Ff

Fruit   F is for fruit.

Fruta   F como en la fruta.

Gg

Gorilla G is for gorilla.

Gorila G como en el gorila.

Hh

Hamburger   H is for hamburger.

Hamburguesa   H como en la hamburguesa.

Ii

Iguana — I is for iguana.

Iguana — I como en la iguana.

Jj

Juice	J is for juice.

Jugos	J como en los jugos.

Kk

Kiwi K is for kiwi.

Kiwi K como en el kiwi.

Ll

Lemon   L is for lemon.

Limón   L como en el limón.

ll

Llamas Ll como en los llamas.

Mm

Mango   M is for mango.

Mango   M como en el mango.

Nn

Nuts   N is for nuts.

Nueces   N como en los nueces.

Ñ

Ñandús   Ñ como en los ñandús.

Oo

Orangutan   O is for orangutan.

Orangután   O como en el orangután.

Pp

Pineapple	P is for pineapple.

Piña	P como en la piña.

Qq

Quintuplets   Q is for quintuplets.

Quintillizos   Q como en los quintillizos.

Rr

Radishes   R is for radishes.

Rábanos   R como en los rábanos.

rr

Rr como en los burros.

Ss

Sandwich   S is for sandwich.

Sandwich   S como en el sandwich.

Tt

Tomato T is for tomato.

Tomate T como en el tomate.

Uu

Uniform   U is for uniform.

Uniforme   U como en el uniforme.

Vv

Vegetables   V is for vegetables.

Verduras   V como en las verduras.

Ww

Windsurf   W is for windsurf.

Windsurf   W como en windsurf.

Xx

Xylophone   X is for xylophone.

Xilófono   X como en el xilófono.

Yy

Yacht   Y is for yacht.

Yate   Y como en el yate.

Zz

Zoo	Z is for zoo.

Zoológico	Z como en el zoológico.

The English Alphabet		**El alfabéto en español** **The Spanish Alphabet**	
Aa	avocado	Aa	el aguacate
Bb	bananas	Bb	los bananas
Cc	coconut	Cc	el coco
Dd	doughnuts	ch*	el chimpancé
Ee	elephant	Dd	las donas
Ff	fruit	Ee	el elefante
Gg	gorilla	Ff	la fruta
Hh	hamburger	Gg	el gorila
Ii	iguana	Hh	la hamburguesa
Jj	juice	Ii	la iguana
Kk	kiwi	Jj	los jugos
Ll	lemon	Kk	el kiwi
Mm	mango	Ll	el limón
Nn	nuts	ll*	los llamas
Oo	orangutan	Mm	el mango
Pp	pineapple	Nn	los nueces
Qq	quintuplets	ñ*	los ñandús
Rr	radishes	Oo	el orangután
Ss	sandwich	Pp	la piña
Tt	tomato	Qq	los quintillizos
Uu	uniform	Rr	los rábanos
Vv	vegetables	rr*	los burros
Ww	windsurf	Ss	el sandwich
Xx	xylophone	Tt	el tomate
Yy	yacht	Uu	el uniforme
Zz	zoo	Vv	las verduras
		Ww	windsurf
		Xx	el xilófono
		Yy	el yate
		Zz	el zoológico

* These four additional letter combinations/sounds are included in the Spanish alphabet: ch, ll, ñ, rr.

About The Author

Sharon Ann Duvernay, Ed.D. was born in New Orleans, Louisiana. She graduated from the University of California at San Diego, received a Master of Arts in Special Education at California State University, Dominguez Hills, along with concurrent teaching credentials in General Education and in Special Education. While teaching in the Los Angeles Unified School District she received a Language Development Specialist Certificate and a Resource Specialist Certificate. She taught all elementary grade levels, bilingually, as well as the first Bilingual Gifted Class in the district. Dr. Duvernay has a Bilingual Cross-cultural Language Development Certificate in Spanish, a Doctorate of Education in Educational Leadership and Change, and an Administrative Credential. She has taught at the University of California at Los Angeles, the University of Southern California, Chapman University, and the Fielding Graduate University in Santa Barbara, California.

Dr. Duvernay lives in Palmdale, California.

www.ingramcontent.com/pod-product-compliance
Lightning Source LLC
Chambersburg PA
CBHW041537040426

42446CB00002B/120